LUMEN

82 -99

10/6

Tiffany Atkinson was born in Berlin in 1972 to an army family, and lived in Wales after moving to Cardiff to take a PhD in Critical Theory. After teaching at Aberystwyth University for some years, she is now Professor in Creative Writing at the University of East Anglia.

She won the Cardiff Academi International Poetry Competition in 2001. Her first collection, *Kink and Particle* (Seren Books, 2006), was a Poetry Book Society Recommendation, and won the Jerwood Aldeburgh First Collection Prize and was shortlisted for the Glen Dimplex New Writers Award. *Catulla et al* (Bloodaxe Books, 2011), her second collection, was shortlisted for the Roland Mathias Poetry Award (Wales Book of the Year) in 2012 and was a *TLS* Book of the Year. Her third collection, *So Many Moving Parts* (Bloodaxe Books, 2014), was a Poetry Book Society Recommendation, and won the Roland Mathias Poetry Award (Wales Book of the Year) in 2015. Also a Poetry Book Society Recommendation, her fourth collection, *Lumen* (Bloodaxe Books, 2021), includes a sequence exploring representations of pain, illness and recovery – work that won the 2014 Medicine Unboxed Prize.

She is the editor of a theoretical textbook, *The Body: A Reader* (2003), and has strong research interests in the medical humanities, especially the history of anatomy and representations of the body, and is currently working on a series of critical essays about 'the poetics of embarrassment'.

TIFFANY ATKINSON

Lumen

BLOODAXE BOOKS

Copyright © Tiffany Atkinson 2021

ISBN: 978 1 78037 530 4

First published 2021 by
Bloodaxe Books Ltd,
Eastburn,
South Park,
Hexham,
Northumberland NE46 1BS.

www.bloodaxebooks.com
For further information about Bloodaxe titles
please visit our website and join our mailing list
or write to the above address for a catalogue

Supported using public funding by
**ARTS COUNCIL
ENGLAND**

Cover design: Neil Astley & Pamela Robertson-Pearce.

Printed in Great Britain by Bell & Bain Limited, Glasgow, Scotland, on
acid-free paper sourced from mills with FSC chain of custody certification.

'Illness is neither an indulgence for which people have to pay, nor an offence for which they should be penalised.'

ANEURIN BEVAN

ACKNOWLEDGEMENTS

Warmest thanks to everyone who has given me help and encouragement, but especially to: Neil Astley, Andrew Cowan, The 'Coven' (you know who you are), Martin Figura, Jorge Fondebrider, Kate Griffin, Sam Guglani, Jo Guthrie, Chris Hamilton Emery, Jonathan Hirschfield, Andrea Holland, Helen Ivory, Gideon Koppel, Andrew McDonnell, Esther Morgan, Sam North, Christopher Reid, Denise Riley, Elisabeth Salter, Rebecca Stott, George Szirtes, Peter Thomas, Deirdre Wilson and Theodore Zeldin.

Special thanks also to Bronglais Hospital, Aberystwyth for allowing me to hang around in May 2014; to the *Medicine Unboxed* organisation for the MU International Arts Prize 2014 for 'Dolorimeter'; to the National Library of Wales for the display of Dylan Thomas's manuscripts in June 2014; and to the Hawthornden Trust for a Residential Fellowship in June 2016.

Thanks to the following publications and online events where some of these poems have been featured: *New Boots and Pantisocracies* (2015), *The Hippocrates Book of the Heart* (The Hippocrates Press, 2017), *English: Journal of Literature and Reviews* (2018), *BuenosAiresPoetry.com* (2019), *Poetry at Sangam* (2019), NCLA *Inside Writing* Festival 2020, *Poetry Wales* (2020) and *Writing Places* (Seagull Books, 2019).

CONTENTS

I *Dolorimeter:* 19 READINGS

11 /ˌdɒləˈrɪmɪtə/
12 Table 8.1: What makes patients anxious about gastroscopy
14 Heroin works
15 Found poem I
17 Accident & Emergency
19 Song of a pain
20 McGill Pain Questionnaire (annotated) please tick
21 Mr Broad's morphine
23 Neuropathy
25 SOCRATES
27 Found poem II
28 A Biblical pain   & an aside on bedside manner
30 Pranidhana
31 A line from the doctor (annotated)
32 Clean windows
34 A bad cold
35 Signs of the body: longitudinal sample at tea break
36 Last
38 The smokers outside Bronglais hospital

II
41 You can't go there
50 The heart it's true looks jaunty
51 Walking with Virginia
52 In this class
53 Mantras
54 The department of small arts
55 Consent
56 Dear Sam
57 It is a very gracious hotel
58 Workshop
59 Panels
60 *There is no sexual relation*
61 Hymn

62   Dog speaks

63   Categories of experience *c*. 2016

64   The poem Kolkata

65   Wire-seller, Lal-Bazar

66   Kalighat

67   Yoga

68   Parable

69   Postscript

70   21 points for a feminist essay on film

72   Burgeon

73   Neighbour

74   Experiment

76   Eggshell

79   NOTES

I

Dolorimeter

19 readings

*With warmest thanks to the staff and patients
of Bronglais Hospital, Aberystwyth*

/ˌdɒləˈrɪmɪtə/

A dolorimeter
is an instrument
used to measure <u>pain</u>
<u>threshold</u> and tolerance.
Dolorimetry has been defined
as 'the measurement of <u>pain sensitivity</u>
or <u>pain intensity</u>'. See *inter alia*: <u>reliability</u>.
We might also call it <u>language</u>.

Table 8.1 *What makes patients anxious about gastroscopy*

58% vomiting   ENDOGEAR CONTENTS
Tubing for EGP 100
Endo – within   Skopeo – to view
Milk-free tea then Mari   for an endoscopy

50% cancer   Some patients like to look at the screen
Hippocrates is recorded as having inspected the rectum
with a candle   Some don't

36% uncertainty   Mr Edwards a pair of dignity shorts
Let's start at the top end   a quickie   For
a couple starting out this is a great home to get stuck into

32% breathlessness Waiting for hospital transport and may have to go at a
moment's notice   looked out of the window
saw the rugby saw the green green grass

26% pain   Embarrassing Bodies
is a way of reaching that demographic
A problem of language (1985)
Everyone is used to it but me

16% the injection   gastro   she said it's gastro   gastro
A laryngectomy cough is the sound of a vixen
far off in the dark   My god
I wanted sedatives I was terrified

15% losing self-control   Clean area: male/female changing
rooms   staff/rest rooms with adjoining
kitchen   I refused radiotherapy

14% duration of endoscopy   Dirty areas: automated
endoscope disinfector double sink/
drainer   work surface with cupboards under
Don't Die of Embarrassment

9% at mercy of others   bad with pro   nounce   ee   ation   especially
Arabic names   *One of the problems*
Andy had to deal with was a party wall
I had a bad time but was well-looked-
after   24 hour use   discard daily
Oh my husband was an angel

4%   death

Heroin works

The consultant's tales fly out around
corners and just before doors swing shut

Like one about a *chronic painer*   one of his first
and abdominal pain being one of the worst things
she was desperate and all of her family   desperate.

In the house the pain hung like laundry from each edge.
You could walk in and feel it flap against your face.
It was thick in some corners like meat

and there was nowhere else to put it.
The mother was smoking Silk Cut back-to-back.
The pain was like television left on loud in a room

that you couldn't get into. The father was busy
and the pain was a baby that no one could find.
The brothers were upstairs   all three   loudly

and the patient herself was glassy and still
just out of her teens with a face of clenched fingers.
It was all like the mouth of a tunnel   where no one

could turn round and no one could carry on either
everyone dazy with fumes. And he the consultant
then such a young man   knew he had to step up briskly

waving the bright umbrella   and drag them the hell
to anywhere that wasn't this. So it was time to try it
he said. And the look on her face and how her eyes

blew open like a door swung wide on a huge sky.
Relief he said   and not for her pain but for a world
restored   as if the house had burst into song or a film

14

where the family sits down to an ordinary breakfast
and the doctor goes on his way   his white power
throbbing   on/off   through his coat.

Found poem I

Notes written by Dylan Thomas while composing his last poem, the unfinished 'Elegy'
to his father.

Oh pain consumed him

           Tired
           Consumed

In one   Pain made him skin & bone &
           ////   spirit ////

                      tired
                      skin & bone
                      and

                      skin soul & ///
                      bone

           Oh, pain

S.   die darkly
             live lightly

                                  love
                                  above
                                  move
                                  gruff
                                  scoff

And Afraid

Accident & Emergency

Anyone claiming that time
is objective deserves a night
in A & E   And there we were

for a thousand years
as the plumbing dried up
the vending-machine un-

invented itself and left
to our wipe-clean seats we
dropped so deep into ourselves

it was another wound
of sorts   Only the smokers
as the doors sucked in / out

strung us to the outside
on a burnt thread   Through
that sea of greenish light

as night cranked on the pivot
of itself   the boy with the appendix
(no bed   nil by mouth)

rose on a private tide
until his pain swayed all of us
The clubbers on their hobbled feet

the sports-day kids   the junkies
ticcing and my father   half-
in   half-out   Where was help

What good our million faculties
The world shrank to the hot
rooms of our hands   Then sea-

change   Nurses flying with their
sails up and a lone consultant
clattering from deep within

the engine of the place   It was
a scene from distant childhood –
drifts of women acting softly

round the patriarch
who moves in glittering belief
This is how the world works

still   my father said
as I shouldered his weight
towards the unthinkable exit

Song of a pain

I was born on a breath like a tumble of notes
She cried out and I scattered

flexing the force of myself through the nerves
like a new god   gathering brilliance

as I spun in time and space
with bright hooks out for landing

How was I ever not here? Impossible
In this garden

I have always been the dark rose
What do I know of my openings

and deaths except this   now
this being airborne like a voice

above her soft ground   drawing tight
so when she breathes I'll swoop back in—

McGill Pain Questionnaire (annotated) please tick

FLICKERING	TICKLISH	ASTRINGENT
QUIVERING	OTIOSE	BURNISHED
PULSING	BLUE	HIGHPITCHED
THROBBING	DESCENDING	ELECTRIC
JUMPING	NETTLING	SHARP
FLASHING	WHISTLING	CUTTING
SHOOTING	PECKING	BUSHY
GRINDING	UNPICKING	ELASTIC
SICKENING	RECKLESS	SKITTISH
SUFFOCATING	FASTIDIOUS	PAROCHIAL
BRIEF	ANALOGUE	QUANTUM
MOMENTARY	LONGWINDED	REGENCY
TRANSIENT	LENTICULAR	DOCTRINAIRE
RHYTHMIC	RETRO	CURSIVE
FEARFUL	NEEDY	TRADITIONAL
FRIGHTENING	ORACULAR	SCANDALOUS
TENDER	TWO-TONE	GRANULATED
TAUT	PYROCLASTIC	SWAGGED
RASPING	ERSATZ	INDUSTRIAL
PUNISHING	ANARCHIC	DEVOUT
GRUELLING	ARTISANAL	NEOLITHIC
VICIOUS	FEISTY	COLONIAL
KILLING	HOLLYWOOD	TRANSCENDENT

Mr Broad's morphine

When it all got bad I couldn't see an end
to it I couldn't see how it would work out.
Am I going to die? I said. The nurse didn't
bat an eyelid. Then

they were wheeling me to theatre bumping
down the old farm track I knew each rut and there
was the farmer sat on the bed with a sheep
and the dog. The dog

was on the floor and he wanted to sell me
the dog. This is what we were worried about.
So we talked it all the way through and when I
got back to the ward

I said Kathy Kathy turn off the fan it
smells of you know. Poo. It smells of shit. But the
smell got worse it was thick like a bandage I
couldn't believe how

anyone could walk around in that. KATHY
I said and looked down into the valley where
there was a music festival I could see
the lights the dancing

and was terrified because they didn't know
about the poo the shit and I was waving
waving standing on the bed and shouting out.
Then it did. It came

exploding through the valley in a thick wave
dreadful awful and they didn't CARE   They were
playing in it swimming and so forth chucking
it around breathing

it in *Iesu mawr* it was the most dreadful
the worst. Look I'm sitting here with tears in my
eyes just trying to tell you. But the nurses
they can make your life

a misery and it won't even you know
be visible or they can save your life. It's
a relationship and if you're some grumpy
old scrote well I tried

to keep my manners even when you know. But
you don't want to hear this let me try again.
That was the worst part and god help me love no
verse can come of that.

Neuropathy

Is it odd
that eighteen months
into his treatment

Dad's neuropathy
   (collateral from chemo
no sensation in his finger-
tips or feet

and irreversible
he cannot do his buttons
sense the dog's fur
   or stay on a bicycle)

subdues him more
than all the Gormenghast
of cancer? He's

an army man
pragmatic as a horse
and he dislikes how I mythologise

It's true
that in his illness
I have found a way of daughtering
that falters as he rights himself

but this is not *King Lear*
nor pain and all its gaudy wagons
but the dusty silence after

First rule   said a triage nurse
   the shouter isn't necessarily
the worst-off   Pain's

a *vital* sign   Look for the one
who's drawn himself in
like a stone   Look

for the one (from convent
Sundays thirty years ago
I've dredged up Father Damien
'the lepers' priest') who

at the story's turn
delivers implacably
   the sermon on *caritas*

with one hand spitting
in the altar candle's
     flame

SOCRATES

Site – *Where is the pain*
        In the violet corners
        Under my tongue
        at the root of language
        At the bottom of my red bag   ringing all hours
        Jesus how can you ask that
                        Here   Here   Here

Onset – *When did the pain start*
        I have thought about this a good while
        My wife says round about the time
        we got back from Corfu   but
        I kept quiet for the first four billion years

Character – *What is the pain like*
        Drama queen   bad Dad
        alien   vicious
        wee shite slinking up to the house
        with *my* fucking keys in its hand

Radiation – *Does the pain radiate*
        But I'm flashing like a cursor
        nail bomb
        permanent terrorist broadcast
                from the bottom of the sea

Associations – *Any signs or symptoms associated with it*
        Mother comes down to the garden in her headscarf
        with a handful of tumours
        tubers
        go get your bucket and spade, my mouse
        and help me dig them in

Time course – *Does it follow any pattern*
      See: history
      See also: structure
      of the novel (post-war)

Exacerbating/ relieving factors – *Does anything change it*
      It is not an economy
      marriage   weather-system
      tight shoe or an untuned radio
      but sometimes I watch
      as it turns on itself like a prom queen
      no one's watching

Severity – *How bad is the pain*
      Let's take everything that's not the pain
      Let's gather that and hang it out in daylight
      can we
      from the dark nail?

Found poem II

*Notes written by Dylan Thomas while composing his last poem, the unfinished 'Elegy'
to his father.*

And loth to sleep, with so much sleep to be   sonnet

////   villanelle

canzone

An old tormented man three quarters blood   rondel
Wearing away to the beat of the /// sea
Will never go <u>out</u> of my mind

Wearing away, and poor but for his pain,

Wound of his life   aloud

shroud

Wearing away   cloud

proved

Caught between two nights   bowed

=====

Poor in all but pain   whined

And Pain was all he had to call his own,
Wound   Though God knows
Wearing away and poor in all but pains.
Dying the dark way* he ---------- pined

distress   He who had
consume
languid   He had not found
starve
waste

* long [DT annotation]

27

A Biblical pain   & an aside on bedside manner

Take Job for example, richly blessed
with wealth and sons and daughters and a wife
who knew her own mind. Job was pure,
content and thence a great man of the East.

Yahweh and the other meanwhile,
in the glitter of the heavenly host were
squaring up. *For have you considered
my servant Job?* God bragged, and so begat

Job's trial of loss on its Hollywood scale:
his smiling children, servants, beasts, and all
the joy and wealth they earned him (one of them,
but which, spared him his wife). Yet Job

held fast. *Naked I came and shall depart*, etc.
Satan spat and rolled a cigarette. *Skin for skin!
Stretch out your hand and strike his flesh and bones,
and he will surely curse you to your face.* So

Job was lanced from inside out with boils.
He squatted in the ashes, hacking quietly
at his poor skin with a shard, and nowhere
for the pain except his own huge burgher's heart.

All in good time Job's friends muster up,
they talk, God pitches in, and commentators
move towards the burden of the book which is
a dialectic masterpiece on why the righteous suffer:

see Augustine. See Maimonides, Aquinas,
Luther, Calvin, *et al.* Much made too of literary
qualities: see Tennyson. But little said of how
the three friends BILDAD, ELIPHAS and ZOPHAR

played their part, for *seeing how great his mortal*
suffering they wept aloud, they tore their robes,
they smeared their heads with ash. They sat with him
for seven days and seven nights and *no one said a word*.

This silence long as mourning, it is anything but action.
Neither apparatus nor a balm. And yet the space
in which Job takes the measure of his hurt, of God,
both sliding wide of language, leaving ash.

Is it the hinge on which the whole tale turns.
Eventually it's Job who breaks the silence
on a hot wing of lament – O thus is Job restored!
though arguably God's reasoning is not, quite.

This is not the point. The three dumb friends,
though never thanked or recognised as healers
(even by themselves) first did that work,
of putting up from sympathy their quiet tent.

Pranidhana

But my Buddhist friend points out that anyone
can exercise compassion
in the face of *suffering*.

The more advanced wish even further joy
to those whose happiness out–
strips one's own by cubits—

those who no more need the dry ship's biscuit
of our *pranidhana* than the stars. Ex-
perimentally, I think

of him all lunch hour, hale and bright and glossy
as Apollo, my superior in most respects
by ratios of roughly

one part sulk to eight parts genuflection;
feel the heart-stone hit
the bottom of that lake.

A line from the doctor (annotated)

We are trying to avoid the word *pain*
It is far too full of itself   This

is less a problem of language
than a problem of belief

Anyone can tolerate a small scratch
Anyone can manage their discomfort

but tug on the root of *peine/*
                        poena/
                                poine
who knows what you might drag up

and blood-feud   judgment   hellfire   torment
these are no longer medical concerns

Keep the language clean and well-lit
Leave its shadows swinging on the gate

Clean windows

Sean   the new department manager
spends all the petty cash
on window cleaners
for these huge panes
six floors up

They all have their foibles
says Pinky   shucking a glove
with a smack   We're in
the main ward   high and formal
as an Oxbridge hall

A trolley turns a corner
somewhere deep and then
as if the hospital
swings downwind
and hangs on its anchor

calm rolls up the jinxy
stairwells to this floor   where
through the hand-rinsed glass
we watch a white van
climb out of the valley

to the new world   What's
a word for how the light
this cold May afternoon
ruffles the blue pleated curtain
behind Mr Mooney

reaching for his tumbler
like a man underwater? I
have   *lumen*   biro'd on my hand
because the nurse who used it
scuttled off before I got to ask

What's a lumen   Pinky?
Just an opening   she says

A bad cold

The consultant has a bad cold
He is like a shot of mercury
that's woken in a glassy tube
Keeps hitting the roof of himself
Textbook   say the office girls
leaving Lemsip on his desk   ad-
justing the magnolias of paperwork

Signs of the body: longitudinal sample at tea break

A cough
a handprint
shrinking from the wiped formica
someone's well-toothed apple core
a damp bouquet of tissues in the bin
my hunger rolling downward like a stone
and spores of perfume in the stairwell
    cough   another cough
        a sniff
                a minor coin
of new shit in the loo's bleached font

Last

I

and quietest day   Janette in reception
who's managing the work of three will *not*
let me help (no clearance)   Out-

patients don't want to talk   they just
want to get out   The TV tells twelve empty
chairs about the trouble with risotto

II

The consultant stops dead and squints at me
over his glasses   Oh   he says   Then later
on his way back through   And what were you
hoping to find here

III

                    A common language I
don't say   But I want him to know that though
it *looks* like all I do is sit around   I'm sitting
with the quandary of how to formulate what's
inside   This is Endoscopy   this man knows about
the inside   You could say we have the same concerns
                                 I say:

IV

I'm fraudulent   in fine health   I have read   a lot of theory
passing the hospital for three years daily on my way to work   I
write about the body   teach *the uses of literacy*   I wanted to be
awkward   out of work   and quiet   with a notebook   somebody
to overhear   three weeks of anonymity   schlepping myself cleanly
in and out   a duffle bag of stupid questions   no one minding if I'm
capable at anything   I listen   sometimes almost touching   almost
It is not much   And I found   I'm sorry   this is contrary to regulations
(pulling from my rucksack) this laminated chart outlining seven shapes
of shit   this cheerful promotional pen emblazoned PROZAC   this glossy
poster saying DON'T DIE OF EMBARRASSMENT

V

Are you capable at anything   he says

VI

I don't know

VII

And language too shuttles between frank
utility and the joy of doing what it pleases
        We're incidental to it after all   A

call for the consultant   Off he goes   I pack
up my notebooks and biros   Someone behind
the frightening curtain is helpless with laughter

The smokers outside Bronglais Hospital

are gods of an old world
The sun thrashes down
                              or the rain
and they weave incessantly their smouldering threshold

From time to time the cool doors part
and one goes in or out
                              with stick or bag
or gown blown out at the back

The nurse in her peppermint uniform
throws them a sneeze   and her ponytail swings
                              The emergency
corridor turns on its squeaky bright wheel

The smokers meanwhile
are proving how all things in motion
                              have first to show up
at the half-way mark   ergo

and by minute degrees
as Zeno might have mentioned
                              had he stopped for a light
outside Bronglais   the cigarette is in principle un-

finishable   So the burnt herb travels for ever
the space between body and ghost
                              The same distance for all of us
and oh   a finger's length   at most

II

You can't go there

The dog and I are mess-mates   significant others   which is healthy or not depending on how you see ecosystems in the round. Child-less not *child-free*   not yet the breezy rhetoric of liberation. Perhaps I will grow into it.

~

You haven't seen joy until you've seen the red dog swimming. Into the river he bowls like a runaway wheelbarrow   seizing the stick with a wriggle of glee. Human joy is rarely so explicit   though why measure feeling by species. Or consider how he tackles his marrow-bone   balancing it between his gold wrists like an ice-cream cone and pushing his tongue into the sweet hole.

~

That the puppy came about the time that B and I began the IVF was just coincidence. Still   there's always someone saying how a childless couple got themselves a dog and   BAM. Oh   folklore.

~

Anyway you don't just *get* a dog a dog's no surrogate for anything he has his own ontology. I know the intricate begats of Otto's pedigree far better than my own and certainly he's not *mine*. First I've vowed to share the dog to death with B   and more profoundly it's a dud the one about man's taming of the wolf. Species theorist and dog-lover Donna Haraway has called our 'upper hand' a case of 'Hegel in the kennels'.[1] Not so fast there Master. Dogs chose us our early settler ancestors. Unlike wolves they learned to override their flight-trigger responses for the riches of our middens and our campfires. Thus she says   we make companion species. Kind.

~

Helpful Pamphlet from the Clinic offers counselling in small-print.
And yet there are so many films about apocalypse and why not watch
the lot of them. Here comes the annihilating light!   a thickening
cone of dark!   the scouring ice-horizon! What an evening ritual.
Overnight you feel your deep self turning like the moon from an
eclipse then wake so very lightly balanced on the present. *This is
everything there is I am ecstatic!* Or   *all flesh is as grass*[2]   I will
not be coming in today.

~

Of the films the one I keep returning to has all the kitsch portent-
ousness of dream. Like dream it burns free of its situational prop-
ellants in a flash. First scene   WHAM   the earth's devoured in
a fireball by a huge rogue planet   flaming debris smoulders on a
rising gyre of Wagner truly it is hard to take but still   there's
something here that calms me   I have watched this scene perhaps
a hundred times.[3] They call the mighty planet 'Melancholia'.

~

Freud   who I love by the way despite everything   unhooks
melancholia from *mourning*   both in the subject's relation to the
lost thing and in where this all gets played out.[4] I find this helpful.
Mourning is good conscious work   a mourner knows exactly what
is lost   it smites like a dropped knife. Bit by painful bit   however
love is wound back strand by strand and slowly threaded elsewhere.
Melancholics work in murkier terrain   though shimmering with
loss they cannot say precisely of what. They are hamstrung in the
halls of the unconscious. Thus a thread of melancholic love can
fester like an ingrown hair   e.g. they're known for long sleeves and
extravagant self-criticism. Herr Freud doesn't see this as humility
but as a dose of hellfire for the 'lost internal object'   though
revenge is wreaked on others anyway through all that shameless sad.
Hell yeah   we're twisty pickles   someone said   to live with.

~

What might one do differently and would one. E.g. in my youth the man called P wanted *babies*   I did not he was a fly-by. But a hot bank holiday a drunken picnic in the woods and   well. A tinny bell rang distantly inside but I forgot it for a good while. He said have the child and give the child to me and I said no no no no no. I have never been so thoroughly deranged. He said   and pulled his phone out   he was going to have me sectioned   and when that failed he proposed. When finally I made a choice between impossibles he sat in the corner of that cool blue room and read the *Telegraph* from cover to crisp cover   yes the *Telegraph*. You've all been terribly professional said he as the nurses regarded me. I walked out as upright as I could my head full   *why*   of models of deportment from the early throes of *Downton Abbey*. Two days after that I ran the Brighton marathon   faintly hoping it might finish me off but it did not   I am no Victorian.

~

In the second sequence of the movie *Melancholia*[5] the Earth returns all leafy and salvific   so the whole disaster can unfold again from ground-level. This we witness through an isolated clan of fucked-up handsome bourgeois white Amerikans. Oh wait   it can't be the apocalypse   not really   not for *them*. And yet we've seen it happen. Gone. All art all feelings all the politics and languages all geography all history and every living creature all that's past present and future. Everything you can think and you can't. Why stick around to watch this happen twice? The film enacts at astral level what the critic Lauren Berlant calls in other contexts   *cruel optimism*. What Buddhists in all contexts you can think of call *attachment to samsara*.

~

Berlant: *a relation of cruel optimism exists when something you desire is actually an obstacle to your flourishing.*[6]

~

43

Object of desire. How casually that cheap balloon phrase floats free of conditions on the ground. And that is no place these days for the building of the old gold dreams   'enduring reciprocity in couples, families, political systems, institutions, markets and at work—when the evidence of their instability, fragility and dear cost abounds'. And yet   since fantasy is how we 'hoard idealising tableaux about how we and the world add up to something'   it proves easier to give an *object* up than to uproot the thick rhizome of wishfulness beneath.

~

Cruel optimism is a melancholy pointed at the future.

~

So from hot to cold relations via ovulation screening bloodwork semen samples acupuncture reflexology nutritionists and relaxation techniques desperate weekends in absurd hotels and lastly   lastly IVF and now we're talking absolute alienation from conditions of production. Pop your panties off and hop up here love. No love no art there at all.

~

Puppy owners have to think of if and when they'll get their dog 'done'   spayed or neutered   family planning. Here comes *Captain Nutsack!* students cried as Otto swaggered down the corridor   a ginger John Wayne   humpy and erratic. But how sad it would be   B said   for him not to sire a litter   never to know fatherhood.

~

Of course the opposite of failure has to be success no matter how circuitous. One door shuts/ another springs ajar   and bang we must   indeed   until it does. Cruel optimism is another phrase for *trying*. If you didn't want it hard enough   you haven't failed

so much as stayed where you deserved   and even if you've failed
you haven't really   you just haven't   quite   succeeded yet. IVF
has much in common with the slippy syntaxes of meritocracy. A
shimmer of manifest destiny held in place by swampy empirical
evidence and a hot core of emotional investment. This also describes
the plot of the film *Melancholia*.

~

POSITIVE THINKING says the nurse across another barrage of
embarrassing procedures THAT'S THE MAGIC INGREDIENT.

~

Letting go then   would mean not just letting go the *object* let's
say   baby   but the bathwater the tub the landing and indeed
the whole rig of the house. The very apparatus that allows you to be
personlike at all. You could try to turn your 'self' towards another
object   only what would you have left to turn and point with.
This perhaps why failure   even when statistically likely   feels
so *catastrophic*. This the situation B and I   I think so   found
ourselves in.

~

I wonder if the dog has a sense of future or whether his now is
just more richly pleated   more tensile than mine. So when I pick
up his lead and he bounces at the back door   past and future are
already folded in the fast-twitch fibres of the bounce.

~

After the IVF failed B got a job in a distant city and I became
primary dog caretaker. Another deep change in the emotional work
of the household.

~

The vet advised I get Otto castrated and I wept. But what about his *reproductive rights!* I said. She peered over her glasses. He's a dog   she said. But still. Companion species. Kind. My clothes are speckled with his hairs and he smells (so I'm told) of my extravagant French scent.

~

Of two sisters in the movie *Melancholia*   one's a good girl. Claire performs the Oedipal exchanges necessary for   say   husband offspring   stables   tailoring   a stoic air of male-directed deference. Younger sister Justine   moody and mercurial   can't make a damn thing stick. On her wedding night   an ill-starred hoo-de-ha hosted by Claire   dear Justine pulls the whole thing slowly   champagne-flute by torch-light   crashing down. Can't help it. Justine's brattish but I like her and her kind. Doesn't melancholia refuse the deal of the exchange   that you accept the substitute for something lost or fathomless   and Justine has a fine grasp of the difference she's an advertising whizz-kid   or she was. She tells her boss to fuck himself over the champagne breakfast   she has strolled in from the golf course having screwed his intern nephew half into the ground. Melancholics could be lovely spanners in the works of the capitalist family machinery   Freud doesn't say.

~

Weeks pass. Sunset grows erratic. Justine limps back to Claire's château like a whipped horse. But she quickens. Planet Melancholia is coming. Nothing but apocalypse can cheer up Justine.

~

At a party trying to explain to a friend of a friend i.e. a stranger why I'm spending Christmas on my own. O small-talk vortex. Surely there's your *family?* says he   glancing at my bare left hand well yes. There is my one eccentric living parent   I'm his sole blood-child and he's been married three times weaving for us both a complex net of family estrangements   but   this is a party.

Time of transition I offer with the little bunny-quotes for ha-ha. Ah   says the stranger raising his glass   well you know what they say   ONE DOOR CLOSES ANOTHER DOOR SHUTS. I smile. Wait. No   I mean… He's flustered. It's okay I say   it's okay and   oh how your slip has let that bloody door slam shut and furnished me an anteroom   an interlude   an impasse. An applause of doors claps shut back through the years   on all my and my father's lost exhausted or in other ways failed partnerships until the last one hangs ajar on a distant nativity   my mother and I   my officer father   our gentle spaniel Remus in the ersatz firelight of a Berlin army quarter. From the narcissistic eye of nuclear family mythology this was peak domestic and emotional attainment. Forty-odd years on the buck stops here. Well since I won't be going anywhere for now I think I'll sit the fuck down. There it is. I raise my own glass. *Cheers.*

~

In *Melancholia* the child invents an apparatus for measuring the movement of the roaring planet to or from the earth. It's an adjustable wire hoop at the end of a pole. He demonstrates   you press one end of the pole to your chest and point it at the sky align the wire hoop at its far end to the planet's circumference and thus read changes in its size/proximity invisible by minutes to the naked eye. Claire's obsessed with it and in the narcissistic slide of all neurosis I identify   how many hundred ovulation tests   the egg is approaching the egg is receding the egg may never come again. Why not throw the damned pole in the fire and sit tight. Chief of the delusions born of having no time left is that there's still time. It's a dark film   only Justine's fatalistic nonchalance is luminous.

~

A friend is in my house   my half-built house. Let's call him J and J is doing me an actual sexual favour. Once I'd said   and why so coy   I just can't do that stuff again   you know   like intimacy though I hate that word it drags a tacky static. J pours himself more whiskey   he's a smiler   only   Otto. Otto doesn't like the shift in ambience. He whines and claws and muscles in and slobbers on our faces. Plants his huge paws on our shoulders from behind. Launches at the bedroom door and bursts the catch. Thrusts his nose beneath the sheets. Meanwhile   dear god   he barks and barks   it's *Carry On* meets *Scooby Doo* it's funny for a while and then I want to cry. This I say   see *this* is the state I have bloody well got myself into. J knows dogs and calms the dog and I make tea by which time Otto's snoring like a drunkard on the night bus. Now it's three a.m. and I'm a raw nerve in the wound of all my failed attachments. Never mind. The ego's a mistake don't take yourself so seriously say the Buddhists   sort of.

~

Nuclear families love to see themselves as 'packs' but really. One of my friend's bitches has a phantom pregnancy she suckles soft toys in a nest beneath the stairs. Dogs alone of all the other animals do this   no one quite knows why. He says that since in any pack just one bitch will be whelping at a time   the others may be triggered into sympathy. Extra 'mothers' to protect and feed the litter. It's a theory.   Not the daftest thing I've ever.

~

There's a run I do on Dartmoor where my dad lives. Miles of curling incline to the high lap of the moor. Once   through a chink of dry-stone granite wall   I glimpsed a raptor with its beak deep in the eye of a carcass   a rabbit perhaps. It must have been ten feet away   and I was moving and my sight is dreadful   did the gap have magnifying properties? Even at the time it seemed contrived   but that is what I saw. And after two-plus years of celibacy *this* is the image that spins in my mind's eye on that fine approaching brink. A deathly little porthole   Oh *Herr Doktor*.[7]

~

48

My dog   whose life is short[8]   is not concerned. You haven't
seen joy until you've seen the red dog swimming. Into the river
he bowls like a runaway wheelbarrow   seizing the stick with a
wriggle of glee. Human joy is rarely so explicit   though why
measure feeling by species. Or consider how he tackles his marrow-
bone   balancing it between his gold wrists like an ice-cream cone
pushing his tongue into the sweet hole.

The heart it's true looks jaunty

how he's sketched it
on our hospital invoice left face-
down for three days in its own red tape,
& language being so

                                        , says Dr Sochala
                    while inking in the dead star of the *embolie*
                              & firing biro arrows hard
                              into your heart's high halls
                                                —*Voilà*

l'obstruction, l'endommage.
Here's someone's fast train
stalled in freakish heat
& gendarmes pushing back

                              a clamour at the tunnel-mouth
                              . Boys on the tracks
                    with lives tamped down in rucksacks
                              also each his own five
                              quarts of blood

past tarp & chain-link
to the inmost districts of the heart.
A woman fastens shutters on the dark
and calls your smallest name.
                    Of course

                              you have no clothes or shoes
                    .The heart meanwhile hears everything
                    . Of course it storms its railings
                              . *Shhhh*
                              says the oxygen-pump
                              to all its citizens

Walking with Virginia

I'm stamping down the promenade
with V who hates the fog has hated
fog since 1912 and as the loose end
of her muffler whips my cheek I think
of your ex that Parisian boneyard looking
down at my shoes and and and Virginia
I say when you and Leonard quarrelled
what did you do with the lean meat
of your heart. My heart she says I rather
think you'll never shake this small town
using words like that so *how* I say
kicking grit at a seagull and she holds out
her hand and the eye I can see through
the floss of her hair is cold and unlit.
What do you want she says you easy
creatures with your plastics and careers
then gets distracted by a couple kissing
in the bandstand but I have her hand
it's dry as a bible please she says don't
be an Austen girl all tears and catastrophic
picnics. Wait she adds but how's your cook
and soon she's squealing through her fingers
at the TV as I fumble pasta into chipped bowls.
God she says what happened then What
happened and she pulls a heap of pebbles
from her pockets so I hold her like a bag
of partridges then lay her tightly what
else could I in the vellum of my bed and
sing the one about the woman crossing
water in the night so soft so

                          black

                              so deep

In this class

let's be clear (1) how I swung from the frayed
end of a Tory line   through boarding schools
and into university at seventeen   that

(2) my tutor took one look and handed me
de Beauvoir   Fanon   Tsvetaeva   thus (3) ensuring
I would never be an army wife   though being

of the thieving bourgeoisie I have her copies still
(4) in my breezeblock office   brightly titled
not unlike in many ways The Officers' Mess

(5) but for being filled in riptides with your kids
who may or may not know freedom from disaster
or be up all night on highs or the thick unreadable

dread I rode at their age   Having just cast votes (6)
over Homer v. the bar   we're at the bar discussing
voice how voice is always elsewhere   something

you must find and lay beside you   like a bearskin
i.e. rarely native or a sweet fit   or indeed the animal
one thought one was but (7) try it on   I say in one

way or another daily   it's a trouble and a right
and (8) they do   they will just keep on speaking up
your kids   who by the way are ok are   magnificent

Mantras

My teacher's name had two short syllables
    They leaned together   ladder against slide
You took the brief climb of the first   its proposition
    then the little drop   its coo   You

couldn't call him by just one part & expect him
    No familiar names   O master
of the old suburban rope-trick   shrugging
    through a gold hoop into Wednesday

afternoons   as straight and true as if
    deceit itself had properties like Photoshop
or maybe   just my own lit gaze became
    a portal he must pass through   In

another district of my life then   I was learning
    meditation   Five hours weekly
for a year   we breathed in   breathed out
    laid down muscle-memory through images

that opened & let go   like   clenched palms
    opening on galaxies   the holy lotus   or
the secret rosy cunts of all the blue-stockings
    I worshipped in baroque un-brilliant essays

or his two insistent syllables   Breathe in
    Breathe out   Atchoo   The little spasm
of that name   How craving can be pushed
    against its fulcrum into weightless non-

attachment   Andrew   All your namesakes
    even now are mantras   Awkward   Still
the open pang of &   then   outbreath   calmly
    common loss rolls on like white flame

The department of small arts

invites you to diminish applications.
you may work in any medium

but are likely to prefer edges and the under-gold.
for example you may listen for the blackbird.

you may have at least one unresponsive parent.
you may be among the peaceniks and the women.

you may drive despite the terror.
you may compliment the cashier's fishtail braids.

you may spot the feathers at the roadside.
you may rearrange the toys in party huddles.

you may give the man your loose change.
you may leave before the hostess is in tears.

should you entertain a huge idea please delegate.
we have no truck. do load your sling with quanta.

we remind you that the grant season blinks twice a year.
consider what has passed through.

> annotation
> milk &
> soft parentheses
> a cardboard plinth
> all secret names
> bespoke
> & little lids that pop up with a *puck*
> a strong historic present
> slow &
> slow &
> slow &
> *wait, let's*

Consent

On the radio it wasn't tyranny
she just said
all the men that have assaulted me in my life
have been nice guys
in a voice that made me think of when your finger
pushes through the cellophane and touches cool meat
FLESH   you think   with your flesh
I was cooking dinner like a citizen
The interviewer was like   woah
I put the chicken down and walked outside
The lawn   the herbs   the ornamental tree
What a sharp and unexpected boredom
Have I   Have I given my consent   O lazy
girl if you don't burn down suburbia
where can you go with a pretty mouth   Who
will you bury in ankle-length yesses and pearls
Mum arises in the backdraft of my cigarettes
though so long into the dark herself she has
poor working syntax and is flat-out knackered
Kid   she spells on the threshold   Even the wind
that cannot read or bone a chicken knows its own mind

Dear Sam

Shit you not I'm in a hammock reading Petrarch
Dazzled water jangles at my slow boat   Rock
rock rock   I move and do not move towards
my love   I sink   The sea's a heavy veil   O

It is a very gracious hotel

and the foyer glitters like a rose-bowl
Nonetheless   once every fifty years or so
there is a minor mix-up at reception   See the man
who leans in and the woman who drops each tired
bag into a pile   The young receptionist is sorry
though perhaps the Shakespeare room might do as well
it's very well-appointed   But the man's voice has unhooked
itself and anyone attuned to such a note   as dogs
hear whistles   just can't help it   up on hind-legs
with a hand out   very   very sorry sir   the chandeliers
suddenly a pair of lit hysterics barely holding it together
and the old upholstery fading just a little   And now man is suffering
the huge indignity of woman bending all her nouse into a touch
She feels the small depletion like a glass dropped on the inside
while the man is slowly pulling down the whole scene   ingrown
valleys   sheepy dusk   the suburbs and the town itself
into his grief   indeed there is no other place to put it
I have been the man and I have been the woman   I have been
the night receptionist revising by the phone   I've been the manager
descending from his ante-room like Moses   backlit   smooth with
platitudes   I've been the chandeliers and windows full of sheep
and green resources   It is my life   a very gracious hotel

Workshop

Now in this ritual a person reads a poem out / J reads his poem
then passes round his poem's little body / Birdsong fills a minute
and O'Hara still hangs in our language from the first hour / No
one ever said that reading was like any other kind of hangout /

and the poem is an incident observed as from the future / It
shrinks a little / Someone picks a word out / albumen / that
tries a bit hard / Okay / J is taking notes / He writes, *a bit much* /
later he writes, *Eggs* / He wants it to say something real / The

whole room wants it like a household polishing its goods up
into Latin / J takes everything down and the margins fill
with conversation like / well, albumen / superfluous / a little bit
disturbing / so he scratches out the thing itself and reads *a bit much* /

*eggs / oblique modes of approaching revelation / male chaffinch /
cut / make weirder / see O'Hara thing / tense / line break / stronger
word for loss / see Hughes / move / Langston not Ted / active use of blank
space / faith in reader / 6 pm grad bar / travels like bits of fire / a keeper*

Panels

Somehow I have crossed the gleaming table and
am on the Panels. What do they think I know?
We have worked on the disposition of chairs
but even so there is a

scythe of us. A glass of water trembles
at the centre. I have sampled its freshness for
such is my power. I've drawn down the blinds.
I am asking the difficult

question. Each jewel swivels brightly in the hot
seat. Tell us. More specifically can you
give us an example. For example, could
you tell us and in what ways

how, precisely, you can excellently both
withstand and dazzle. Thank you. Viewed from space
we are impartial as a cyclone or a great wall.
Please. Take all the time you need.

O diffidence. O fluster. O the 5-point
plan. O impenetrable young men. You may
now retire and pace the afternoon while we're
apportioning the good cuts.

As from confession, one may leave these blinded
rooms embarrassingly close to tears. But we *made*
the day's work's weird vow, to try always, almost,
to accomplish some right thing.

There is no sexual relation

(*Jacques Lacan*)

And the lime tree flings out such
a thunderhead of seed
   a god is withdrawing o did one of us forget

thy gold thread twitching and thy net of fairy-lights through everything
My fingers come back looped with glitter
   & I look up
   from my little house of paperwork

The manager with sharp teeth like a kindergarten devil
   's at his counting desk
   deploying words like *compartmentalise*

Of course desire loves a small enclosure
   and its glammy way with surfaces
   I can't help that

I'm just a slow blink in a shaft of light
that plants its jewel in my toadish forehead
   Well
   was I ever a woman of sound sense

It's my turn to speak I think
   I'll tell them I'm not in today
& fold myself down in the ticklish grass Yes

see my pale hand spring out and my tacky tongue
   that flickers on the quick &
   slippy ling o

Hymn

Red dog shitting
plants his four stars in the grass
and up goes the tent of himself
his tail pegged out
his eyelids fine and private. And I think
       so that's how we do all things with the body.
Here he is.
He lifts a gold wrist like a debutante.
I look at him and know the eye emits a shaft of sticky particles
       and these have formal consequences.
When he hunts in any case I'm lost to him.
He spins on the horizon
       heads/ tails.
Smooth your hand along the dog. He likes that.
If in dreams sometimes I do my red dog harm I wake in thick tears.
If my dog lies like spilt honey
I stretch across the carpet breath-to-breath and watch his yellow eye
       a trapdoor in and out of which some small hot thing is always bolting
flick and grow still.
May I never get over the slapstick of the red dog swimming.
When high wind is the red dog's cinema he shakes.
Only when my dog is quite exhausted
will he push his India-rubber
heart into my palm.
       It jumps.
When friends say look
you know he's not a substitute
do they think I'm an idiot. He chooses daily
       and I rise or don't rise and he takes me.

Dog speaks

What my russet hunt-dog says
    curled in the cream of my bed
        like a worm in a nut   is that   it's me
            wanting discipline   *What's this*

he groans   with one eye rolling up
    and tail flicking lizardly   Where are your boots
        and your teaching voice   why make me
            lie for you   This isn't business   there

isn't a blizzard   and nothing is wrong
    with your forked walking-parts   I don't know
        why you droop so   why   you
            smell so like a bin-fire after rain   What's

this slow extinction   Light yourself   Be lit
    rise up   and mistress   Claim your right
        to push yourself into the world
            so I can sprint my golden loops

or put a collar on and walk   yourself
    the slow length of whatever reeks of grief
        then shit right on it
            and be done   Don't take me

for a heart   some sempiternal human heart
    all struck and gormless   I am short-lived
        horny   huge of whim   your counter-
            weight   Will pull hard every

time and not be told   Though you must try
    like any little talking-god   as I
        must dumbly quite like any
            better self   ignore you

Categories of experience *c.* **2016,**

summer of acute millennial ripening. See
low-grade dread, a horror of authority, a good time
for experimental love. A new taxonomy. *The voice*
as effective defense against personal swamping,
said my younger and more brilliant friends, but
I am the archivist. *Name your state and dwell in it.*
This is personally efficacious; I have found it to be so.

1. DANK.   Habitual and scrolling and inert.
I cannot move, the child says in the dreadful corridor
that keeps on lengthening. And no place I can put this down.
A dull choice. Nothing wingéd. Kindness rolls off. Walks out
in the rain with no coat. So what. Quality of toxin in the unlit
sky. Should look into my heart but it's a gang bang in there.
>> Cautions aerobic activity, radical self-care.

2. SPICY.   Inflaming! O ravishment.
When to look is something that involves the whole skin
and the space between two skins is tensile like a good verb.
You are a *meteor* how did you ever think otherwise! As in
airborne politics! As in heady spend of new love! All my diamond
sides at once! A quality of bladedness but hot and held dear.
>> Cautions humility, radical self-care.

3. PURE.   Salvific. Talismanic. From the soul a flutter
as of bunting. Actual soul! the poor hacked wing.
Conservative but songlike all the same. Stand in the quad
with the sun on your forehead and no enemies. Mother
turns from a dish of strawberries in 1982 and fingers her headscarf.
Sweetheart. Nothing's lost. O don't you just fly home. Quality
of high fine distant bell. Fresh pages. Hearts. Clean air.
>> Cautions irony, radical self-care.

The poem Kolkata

Amit too   I read   between landings
has considered poetry's irrelevance

Like certain genres   certain cities too
become unviable at certain points in history

Just look at poetry   A tale of near-extinction
O   give me any city that's unviable

and push me out in just what I stand up in
Here on the holy-day quayside

I can only move anywhere at the molecular level
A mote of me jangles with the bright girls up the temple steps

Another rises on a drift of puja smoke
Another bombs a couple's grinning selfie with its weird eye

One part strips & wades into the river
and a bit of me dissolves into the marigolds   A fragment

sizzles off the skillet on a mustard seed
Another shatters from the ferry bell   alighting

on a lolling dog who twitches   & rolls over onto
bits of me that burnt down to the ground a century ago

Another million bits fly out   attached to kites   not going
anywhere   like most joys   like a lot of language actually   like this

Wire-seller, Lal-Bazar

          who smiles from the kerb
like a man loosed from thought   who
when he feels its small tug   will turn slowly   fit his spectacles
& from the tangled afternoon   pull down
between his fingertips   its single filament

Kalighat

Sarah brings Kali
Fierce in her embroidered shawl she sticks her tongue out
From the temple she has carried in insurgence   somehow
Women all   we measure the distance in silence
between power   and what passes in the speaking life   for power

Yoga

Early-morning gym-companion/ business-man/ mid-
forties/ white shirt pressed and hanging by the showers/
folds/ unfolds himself like something being born/ still
nine parts liquid one part hurt/ he brings the body stretching
into light/ We nod and smile/ I'm chugging out my tenth mile
on the treadmill/ You go very far he says/ yes far indeed/ but
tell me can you bend

Parable

Arnab and Shonali feed us
sweet fish steamed in leaves with mustard seed

I cast aside my awkward knife and fork
to suck my steaming fingers   Now I'm not one

to discourse on the authentic but THIS FISH
Shonali says that all Bengali mothers make this

Arnab grins   ask anyone   All week I pester women
with my notebook
                    Never mind   says Paramita

when in Norwich six months later I attempt
by way of welcome   fish *katuri*   with a sullen Nordic cod

and mustard from our claggy fields   A boon! our guests say
for the cats   & thus we all decamp for lunch

at the White Horse   George cross and signed pic of Prince
Charles above the bar   but nonetheless the best roast

east of London   so   implausibly   come Spring I find myself
once more on a Kolkata rooftop eating canapés   what *luck*

until the deputy-high-commissioner's wife takes me aside
& says   the fish!   Oh fuck   a diplomatic incident   I think

but really she just wants to say it's all about the seed
which is a mother's true advice   Did no one show me

and she leads me to her kitchen
                              where the massed historic
city leans in   on a woman twisting mustard seeds
in greaseproof   All its horns   and all its flowers   blaring

Postscript

Almost I don't go
      because of a family grief and in winter of some kinds
it's hard to imagine
      a whole other continent
Don't be absurd   says my sensible friend   just step over your-
      self

21 points for a feminist essay on film

1. Something small to say and mostly us to say it.
2. We gather dessert spoons in sticky bouquets.
3. We hear disturbance in the basement

and still we take a candle and go down.
4. We're innocent, if only to ourselves
and want to know the strangeness of our houses.

5. No one breathes until the hemlines go up.
6. Off with our glasses and, oh my, we are delivered
to ourselves like roses. 7. It's the softness

of our bodies. 8. It's all of us laid end-to-end
in a moebius strip of skin & celluloid
that kicks the whole shebang off. 9.

We know when to run by the state of our shoes.
10. If everyone's shoes are sweet we stay. 11.
We may come like someone's pulled a rip-

cord from our bellies and go, YES. Or
12. A lawyer enters. E.g. *did we say no
in the way Plato himself would say no?*

13. Here's our archive of equivocal sounds.
14. The original problem of course is Mother.
15. Or The Workplace. 16. Anyway, to do with

mothers or employment will be why some guy's
still creeping up our shady stair like black mould.
17. He'll call it retribution and they'll count this.

18. So we work real hard to be good astronauts
and cyborgs. Lining up our gleaming corsetry
across the world's bridge! 19. Sister, warrior,

this hypothesis will oust us from the family.
20. Never mind, it's only true in movies.
21. Will someone press the little button—

Burgeon

flowering itself is a sign of distress

DENISE RILEY

No woman likes to go directly out from crying
only sometimes must   I say this as a plain one
well-built   working   this is not an act of rhetoric

who's done her shopping raw of heart and barefoot
Taken meetings as the full pietà   So what   one is not
an engine or a hockey-captain made for roaring   and

besides   who looks   well mostly no one   Only
who   Some dogs   and men in their wolf-suits
always with the same white smoke of pheromone

Well   rather be a mommet in a bad hat   rather
have the door swing in your face than wonder
if the root of all attraction is distress   That flower-

girl you hauled up from the pavement   slightly roughly
for her own damn good and pushed out in your good dress
Save her rosebud eyes   her waxy cheek   Push on   O lacrimosa

Neighbour

This is how the boy walks \
    leaning back against the gaze of anyone
Exhilarant in neon with his flashback
    eighties headband   from the Viking road
towards the new estate   taking a line
    like a striding graffito through PLEASE
DON'T WALK ON THE GRASS   and wreathed
    in sweet smoke like a thurifer   Mostly
I'm putting out bins or waiting for the dog
    to squat   nothing transcendent   tho
his posture makes a brief hypotenuse
    of silence   When the hound leaps up
at something private in his heraldry
    the undergold is momentary   daily

Experiment

in which you sit a piece of firewood in the good chair
knock two gleaming tacks in for expressiveness
and wait to fall in love with it.
Now back to work.

The heart bumps on its bottom stave
all morning through a steady mash of typing*&%*%.
Well it's not done so much *inner work* it speaks
neat cliché that's a fair start.

Will it pick apart your every scattered look
or nick the bloody car-keys come back drunk go
sorry sorry bite your ear and rub up like a goat?
No it's a real gent.

Outside all the office-workers vaping in their Christmas
hats. Your phone is off and buried in the dog-bed. Dog
for once is unperturbed so mild a courtship. Kind wood.
Up you look in thanks

a quick intensity like sunlight through a spyglass
and behind the sunlight all that tilting unlit
weight of space the self. A place
no one can be for long

without the very bones dissolving what a din of
propositions. Work is something hobbies also may be
beneficial but the constellating sweet hormonal twinkle
that's a real knack.

What's this distant beating up of atoms
like the butter coming in a crock of shook milk? Shake it
you have one expensive ornamental jar the body.
Hold out all your binding fats.

Look at this the late sun pulling down its shades
on love or something massy like it. Bless
your sturdy grain and piquant little knots
your ringéd history

and carbon-heavy silence. How your bright tacks
pulse like muted stars! It's time to light the fire my love
for this is how such learning must be got but O
King Log   King Log

Eggshell

Up the slowly gleaming conch of staircase
David inches   pot and brushes   at the threshold
        Who will keep the dog at bay
I'm cross-legged in the bedroom with my laptop
saying Otto   Otto   lie down   doorframes
are a careful work   The brush flicks   David's mouth
        is soft and open slightly
like a creature surfacing   I'm working also
for the rest to fall away   O luxury
        to pay a man
for hands that would be sound in any kind of dark
and not be always spoiling   O my deadline
        Otto snores
his bevelled bronze head heavy on embroidery   How
full of air the songbag of each body's quiet
business   barely lit   a screen-saver Vermeer
        Nothing else   The radio downstairs
A woman's voice tugs back and forth   *disaster*
breaking on the stairwell   Breathe we on   so putting
down no weight at all   earth's curve inside   between

NOTES

You can't go there (41)

1. Donna Haraway, *The Companion Species Manifesto: Dogs, People and Significant Otherness* (2003).
2. Richard Wagner, *Tristan und Isolde* (1859).
3. 'For all flesh is as grass', 1 Peter 1: 24-25.
4. Sigmund Freud, 'Mourning and Melancholia' (1917).
5. Lars von Trier, *Melancholia* (2011).
6. Lauren Berlant, *Cruel Optimism* (2011).
7. 'So, so, Herr Doktor' from Sylvia Plath, 'Lady Lazarus' in *Ariel* (1965).
8. 'Peace / they say to the dog whose life is short' from Jean Follain, 'The art of war' in *130 Poems*, tr. Christopher Middleton (2010).

The department of small arts (54)

From a slip of the tongue heard in a faculty meeting.

Categories of experience, *c.* 2016 (63)

From conversation with Sophie Robinson and Fern Broome Richards.

The poem Kolkata (64)

Italicised text from Amit Chaudhuri's *Calcutta: Two Years in the City* (Union Books, 2013).